Jam

Jam

Poems by

Joe-Anne McLaughlin

Introduction by

STEPHEN DUNN

THE AMERICAN POETS CONTINUUM SERIES NO. 65

BOA Editions, Ltd. ▪ Rochester, New York ▪ 2001

00 01 02 03 7 6 5 4 3 2 1 FIRST EDITION

Publications by BOA Editions, Ltd.—a not-for-profit corporation under section 501 (c) (3) of the United States Internal Revenue Code—are made possible with the assistance of grants from the Literature Program of the New York State Council on the Arts, the Literature Program of the National Endowment for the Arts, the Sonia Raiziss Giop Charitable Foundation, The Halcyon Hill Foundation, Starbucks Foundation, as well as from the Mary S. Mulligan Charitable Trust, the County of Monroe, NY, and The CIRE Foundation.

See Colophon, page 86, for special contributors in support of this book.

Cover Design: Geri McCormick
Art: *Phoenix* by Martha Ward, courtesy of Constance Ashton Myers
Interior design and composition: Valerie Brewster, Scribe Typography
Manufacturing: McNaughton & Gunn, Lithographers
BOA Logo: Mirko

LIBRARY OF CONGRESS CATALOGING-IN-PUBLICATION DATA

McLaughlin, Joe-Anne.
Jam: poems / by Joe-Anne McLaughlin; introduction by Stephen Dunn.
p. cm. — (American poets continuum series; no. 65)
ISBN 1-929918-04-6 (pbk.: alk. paper)
1. Women — Poetry. I. Title. II. American poets continuum series; vol. 65.
PR9199.3.M42435 J3 2001
811'.54 — DC21   2001016180

BOA Editions, Ltd.
Steven Huff, Publisher
Richard Garth, Chair, Board of Directors
A. Poulin, Jr., President & Founder (1976–1996)
260 East Avenue
Rochester, NY 14604
www.boaeditions.org

NYSCA

NATIONAL
ENDOWMENT
FOR THE ARTS

For Hayden

Contents

Jam

Introduction

In her wonderful book *Jam* — a title evocative of jazz and trouble,
Joe-Anne McLaughlin pitches and tunes her poems to a wide
range of emotional experience, often in the same poem blending
the tawdry, the playful, the ruefully sublime. Though her subject
matter is indeed often troubling, what I find myself admiring is
how her syntactical and musical gifts (McLaughlin's Jazz, I
might call it) regularly make what's troubling aesthetically plea-
surable, and how they mitigate bold claims.

In "Abishag's Brag," for example, she dares to conclude with,
"One night of me / and a fellow would / be lonely / all ways." The
choice of "all ways" as two words is typical of how McLaughlin's
use of syntax can disarm us. It delimits the "brag" while height-
ening our sense that we're in the presence of a poet interested in
getting the most out of her language. Here's a poet who knows
how to be both bold and sly.

She's no less bold in the powerful "Loose Children," though
she employs different tactics. With tactile and visual precision,
she writes, "... her body bared and pressed / to its warm damp
planks, the dock / creaking as it heaved beneath her, bleeding
creosote — the heavy sexual reek / of creosote and bay and rot." A
few lines later, though, she abstracts the moment for us, going
beyond the visceral: "Here was a Vanity so thorough it excluded /
Impatience or Envy." Such moves, carefully timed, occur through-
out the book and show McLaughlin's ability to be inside and out-
side her subjects, at once renderer and examiner.

Her ubiquitous Abishag poems appear in every section but
the fourth, and serve as tonal and musical counterparts to the
graver demeanor of some of the other poems. But rarely, even in
the most somber of moments, does she render the somber
somberly. Syntax and line breaks, her fondness for paradox, the

occasional pun—all manage to enliven claims that might otherwise ask for our sympathy.

The fourth section, with its edgy, affirmative love poems, is perhaps my favorite, the poet facing hard facts with a clear-eyed compassion. "Evening Star" is especially beautiful. No verbal hi-jinks here. The eloquent simplicity with which she manages senti-ment reminds me of what William Carlos Williams was able to do in his later work.

I know for a fact that this book has been a long time in the making. There's a sense that McLaughlin has lived her poems, but also has lived *with* her poems, and that is in part why *Jam* distinguishes itself. It is a most impressive achievement.

— STEPHEN DUNN

Part One

Introit

For Mary

Your call comes and I'm off,
as always, this time by train
and, yes, the weather is rotten
and the train breaks down
as they so often do these days;
out my window, a tenement
torched, its windows broken like faces
with here and there a mattress
thrust out: great burnt tongues.

Home Sickness

As if to the scene of a crime, she returns
to her family home, always to create
the same neat corner she required
as a child; she comes bearing steel
brushes, roach powder, bleach — to clean
the old place quiet.

Though the wild, sickly father is long dead,
though the mother still holds true
as the Second Law of Thermodynamics,
housekeeping in reverse,

she returns
holidays, birthdays, divorce, minor
illness, love of family, any
pretext, as if no home of her own
can right the original mess,
as if there were no statute of limitations
on a child's disgrace, no end to her vengeance.

Black Irish Blues

1.

*You mighty beautiful, but you gotta
die someday.*

TRADITIONAL BLUES

Already this tremor in my hands —
like my father's toward the end
when he couldn't steady his fork
long enough to get his food down clean
let alone get down on his bass,
or so his common-law widow said.
It was another one of those last
chances the Musicians' Union gave him,
and I don't know who got his bass
out of Bob's Friendly Loaner for him
that time, unless it was Buzzy,
the trumpet player, who is dead now
too, they say. It was a beauty
of a beast anyway. Grand,
not like the electric jobs
these glamor guys play; only unhandy
as a coffin or a crucifix to haul.
But we hauled her, the twelve blocks
uptown to the Black Orchid. Had to,
and in the pouring rain, because
same as always Daddy'd shot
the cab-fare on stuff. But wasn't he fine,
really in there, those first two sets?
The way he played that box
made me think if a penis could speak

9

it would speak in Bass. Only
then he began missing, worse and worse
(nodding out, is what they call it),
until midway through the third set he crashed—
bass, stool, and all—smack down
on the bouncer's classy date.
Awful. Sure. Only same as always
nobody could afford any trouble.
They packed us into a taxi, and Daddy
was straight enough by then, at least,
to cry. And it wasn't long after, I
got sentenced to the Good Shepherd Home
for Troubled (meaning "wayward") Girls, and next
I heard, he was busted in Miami
for possession. Then he was dead. Now
already his tremor's shaking me,
the single record he left.

2. ELEGY: OUT OF THE PIT, LIKE MUSIC

It didn't rain. It couldn't
gloom as it had his agelong days;
rather the day bloomed and flew,
bluebirds and bluets on every grave.
And shine? A few shades brighter
than ever he could stand, or any of us
when low can bear. Take
the bluest moments of your life,
one Good Friday after another,
Stormy Monday, The Second Flood,
and no change forecast. You knew
(and from lick one) where his music
came from; and I don't mean

from the heart, not that,
nor from no music school either,
but scared up from the glands, like sweat,
and from the tear ducts
and from the dried out cock
doomed yet blowing against all sense
kisses back at puckering death.
You knew, or rather your own doomed
innards knew, and the knowing
trembled through you and ached
so that you didn't know whether
to clap or to gasp.
Understand, for one thus damned,
death is nearly a resurrection.
Understand, it killed me just the same.

Nearly

It was Suzy, the slight
long-haired one who worked
the register nights,
and was dying—who could say
how long? The way she'd chirp,
preen, twittering
like any young person
with a life to live,
only pleasanter, a little
sweeter than most; and then nothing,
except I admired her smile
on occasion, and two weeks after
her funeral, when my doctor
said, "Don't worry, honey,
only loose women get that
kind of cancer," how my foot slipped
loose from the stirrup and nearly
kicked him in his fucking teeth,
which is what a foot does best
when one lacks courage for speech.

Abishag's Brag

Girl, in my foxtails
and fishnets, I was all
city. Exotic
as a Vatican
bagel, accessible
as Port Authority.
I wiggled, lightning
would fork,
sidewalks buckle,
wrong numbers ring,
Earth speak. I was
so out of this world
gorgeous men had to
use raincoats and
boilermakers
for protection.
And cool?—Sister,
I was Antarctica Express.
One night of me
and a fellow would
be lonely
all ways.

Ms. Murphy, To You

Sure. I was drinking.
Shots with beer chasers,
my usual, only it wasn't
the liquor so much as the heat
and the fumes coming off
the old man beside me
that reminded me of my Granddaddy
Pat—that prize fighting,
tap dancing libertine
who named his taproom Liberty
after a race horse—
those wild Irish lies of his
that would time and again drive
my good lace-curtain Grandmother
to her knees: telling my sisters
and me how the Irish in the old country
dyed bad men blue, so that morning
I found him dead, I cried,
"Quick, Grandpa's been bad,"
so I'd come to think of my life as half
vaudeville act, of liberty
as a taproom in a rough neighborhood
like this one, where some hood
can walk off with my change,
and I can afford to close my eyes,
to walk home blind drunk,
feeling godawful rotten for all of us.

Practice

So light her tent
a child could carry it,

her child, the one she'd take
with her if she chose

to go anywhere. At times
she felt so light-

headed, as though almost anyone
dashing or kind

or pretending to be kind
might carry her away.

Hours on end took place
under a kind of

light rainy sleep
until something would break

and there she'd be: pulling up
her skirts to hide her face.

                          Later
she'd land as if by parachute

into the fresh-open-arms
of another dreamer,

and without even leaving the house.
She chose not to leave

the house. Beyond it
all the wrong things worked.

Existentially Speaking

You say eating is pointless,
which is to say life is

pointless, which is a point
we have always

agreed on. And so,
if eating can be no more

or less meaningless
than not eating, given

that dying is as pointless
as living, existentially

speaking, of course:
why not
dig in?

Ancient Francesca

Girl, it's taken everything in me
just to keep myself breathing.

Half then all our chickens
picked off by coyotes, the pig gut
he salted with strychnine,
meant for coyotes, eaten by his own
dogs, the burial of the dogs
useless against the coyotes,
the reburials, the coyote hunters
shooting our goats, his stallion
breaking its leg, startled
by something that looked like
a coyote, the shooting of his stallion,
the burning of its carcass
and in the rain, burning, burning
for days, him taking to mint gin,
turning on me with a shotgun,
that night giving me a hand gun,
locking himself in the storm cellar;
I tell you I ran, ran outrunning
the coyotes, ran and told no one.

Please, please don't ask me anything.

Prison

It could be an ivory tower.
Don't they call us ladies,
serve us breakfast in bed?
Only these Girl Scout uniforms
we wear, and the toilets
without seats, so tasteless.
Nights, all the things we
never knew we loved
getting even with us: the ladies
searching magazines for pictures
of their children, pillows,
pearl toilet seats, houses
they've lived in, cartons
of whole milk, men they've lived
without, things like that;
then there's me knotting sheets
in my dreams, lowering myself
hand under hand, never surprised
when I land that I've landed here;
and last night, Theresa,
whom we never call Terry,
who can no longer remember the name
of the man she murdered,
sticking her arm in my face,
demanding I slit her wrist,
so tasteless, and there was her wrist
and the razor in my hand and me
saying, honey, if it was anybody else,
and cutting into her wrist
like it was the neck of a chicken,

because she was that stupid;
because if I hadn't been born
with full lips and red hair,
I would have been a nun;
because if we have to be evil,
we should remember it, that's all.

Abishag Enjoins Her Cats to Eat

After John Skelton

Come now, old ladies, eat up.
Eat up.
Come now, old ladies, eat up.
Once it was tenderloin medium rare.
For you, sweet cream and calf's liver.
Ho! HO!
For you, sweet cream and calf's liver.

Alas, for the tastes prosperity fostered,
Our hour of picking and choosing has sped.
Alas, for the cream of the cream.

But come, old girls, we must eat.
Must eat.
Come, old girls, for our strength.
Though these victuals be not to our taste,
Though this crow sticks hard in our teeth,
I warrant it's filling enough.
Ho! HO!
I'm assured it is filling enough.

Time we heeded our belly's long plaints,
Time we eschewed our palate's dictates.
Was I a beauty? Now I wash plates.

Picky, picky,
That's what men said, always
Too good for scraps. Well eat

Or don't
As you like, my dears. If not today,
Tomorrow no doubt shall find us
Less particular or dead.
Ho! HO!
Shall prove us less delicate or dead.

Alas, for the tastes prosperity fostered.
Our hour of picking and choosing has fled.
Alas, for a nip of cognac.

Off then, my pets, to nap.
To dream.
Off then, my pets, to our dreams.
For me, a shrimp hollandaise if you please.
For my kitties, a freshly canned tuna.
Ho! HO!
For our friends, a *potage au grease.*

Part Two

Hush

There was a silence
they spoke in:
the deer and the beggar.

The deer
grazing the berm
of the Garden

State Parkway,
the beggar working the odd
last passenger
back at Port Authority,

their language
a quiet that did not say
thank you or wish

you luck, their speech an
argot of silences
saying cold snap
ahead, saying expect no

help from any party,
saying prepare yourself.
Think what you will.

I heard them plain,
as if my hearing
had tapped
an emergency channel, a kind

of underground dog-
whistle frequency,
only those

of us animals
in desperate trouble ever
can reach.

Complicated

For Mary and Art

Like at the rest home, this old vegetable
farmer name of Yank Burns, calling me by his dead wife's
name, calling sweet Alice this, sweet Alice that,
and then steady refusing to eat except on

my shift, meaning of course I couldn't quit
if I wanted to, and Christ—who didn't?
What with the shit wages and urine smell
so cruel somedays it'd like to blister the skin

off your eyeballs. And if you could hack that,
there was the dayroom all the time rigged out
like a funeral parlor. No kidding. Grave baskets
and whatnot, wake flowers, (you've seen them)

long-stemmed fancy arrangements
in cheap baskets, sashed like Miss America
contestants, only instead of a Miss
Nevada or Jersey or Texas or Kansas

you'd get REST IN PEACE, over and over.
Now you talk about creeps; and those old timers,
sitting there, joints sealing, stiffer
by the minute, fat good it did them—good

riddance maybe. But does anybody listen?
So finally one night my car skids sideways

into a tree—you see this scar? Three weeks
I'm on leave and sure enough they had

old Yank packed off to the VA inside
the second week. Force feeding him,
I betcha. Gone, anyway. So I quit—
five years ago this May, and you know

what? Call it fate, which it ain't. Or call it
psychology, which it probably ain't either,
but I haven't held a steady job since.

Abishag Confronts
Her Mirror After a Stroll

A woman without teeth
should not leave her room
or if she must
let her keep moving.

If she loiters anywhere
yes even about the cathedral steps
she should be asked
to move on.

And she should move on.

None of this nonsense about the past.
No more of this breaking into tears.

On Instinct

I have known a stallion
in the fury of his sex

snap his hobbles and flatten
half a corral fence,

who would trample any
creature, beast or man

or immortal, you name it, who chanced
between him and his mares.

I have known a stallion
in a misery of instinct

break for a pasture,
not for freedom but the pasture,

where he ran his feeble colts
breathless and would have run

them lame. I have seen the stud
who would use his hooves,

who would use his teeth,
who would humble the proud male bellies

of his offspring with kicks,
if it were not, my son,

for mothers, for their opposite
equal madness.

Bad Medicine

So it's back to poison, is it,
my beloveds?—lethal injections, mainlined
hemlock: no blood, no bother.

Hemlock? Come on, my dear,
you say: there is no Socrates
on our death rows. And doubtless

you are correct, for though a radical,
Socrates was neither poor nor black.
It's always better to suffer

an injustice, he said, than to inflict one,
and he would not recant
but put his life where his mouth was,
taking his medicine.

Rather

While they are ill let us leave that one last clump
in the cat box undisturbed for them
to witness, or that corner
of the bathroom mirror uncleaned;
let the flecks of toothpaste accumulate
there in flocks for them to notice,
so they cannot be missed, as we assist them
at the toilet or during their towel baths;
whatever their former duties,
let us do them, yes, but not nearly so well
as they did when well. So, too, let us not
assume our grown children despise us
when they leave that last bit of painting
or yardwork unfinished or undone, though
we've long since paid them; rather
let us understand how much our loved ones
still need us to want to need them.

Across the Green

For A. Garcia

From house to compost heap and back takes years
here in the repository of my country's pastoral dreams
— April snow soaking already saturated fields,
making the same limestone glue, the same poor
people's cement, stomped and scraped against
the same uneven floorboards of farmhouse mudrooms.
If we dream at all, it's of personal reforms — full body
bootstraps, four-wheel-drive feet.

Without the yeoman farmers of New England
America would swiftly become the Paris
of Marie and Louis, *a people bereft of any sensibility*
except for sin and suffering, or so Thomas
Jefferson said. Downhill at the Legion, once more
we exchange the stock intimacies
of rural complaint, *too wet, too wet,* while later
across the green, we'll pack the church
basement, which can barely contain the crowds
that turn out for A.A. Which virtue was it, tell us again,
nature was supposed to confer on those who lived
close to the land and its creatures, their cheeks
resting on the flanks of beasts they milked by hand, their ears
pressed close as if listening? — pink-ribboned milkmaids,
strapping indentured servants, sporting on the green! Soon
the ground will have thawed fully enough to bury
this winter's dead. Those with any brains got out
long ago, it's said. As for us, it was always too late to go West.

Psalm of Ramona

...and there was none
to bury them.

PSALM 79:3

The jays' Cleer-Cleer
Come dawn of the day
Is a drill in my ear.
Come stun of the day
My head is an ear
Full of pain trees
Where the dawn-jays drill,
Cleer-Shrill Cleer-Shrill,
After my night full of No
Without one wink of,
Because I am the troddenest
Of down creatures
On God's cruel earth.
You hear me up there:
Me-Me Me-Me?
—Thy monster hath need
of Thee still.

Emergency Measures

For Mary

And if her bath water still
bubbled in gasps or foamed
all over her like a mouth,
she could always switch to showers,
just as she now ate her eggs
scrambled rather than up. What else,
with women all over town
turning up strangled!
Besides any day now
they would catch him—and then,
as her husband always said, they would fry him.
That would be that.

Only him? How could one be
certain it was a man? She looked
at her husband.
Now he was a man. He could still
eat his eggs up, and if the paper's
latest accounts shook him
no more than the Braves' last defeat,
she knew that was how it should be.
Baths were womanish anyway
and that ketchup bleeding
from the corners of his mouth
really meant nothing at all.

She could watch more TV.
She could cook something special for dinner

and if her pantyhose continued to twist
in her hands like a weapon?
Well, that was the thing about murder
as opposed, say, to cancer:
not that murder made less sense but that
it was more personal, more human.

Was it this morning? She'd see,
he said: As simple
as a water pistol yet as lethal
as a bazooka. The perfect gal's
weapon. He'd slid
the gun case past the sausage.
"Hell why wait till Christmas?"

So thoughtful of him, really.

Loose Children

Those summer afternoons when the man who took only boys
    would take her brothers for rides in his cruiser: out on the bay,
        always too far
for them to swim in, she swam alone near shore, dreaming
    the underwater dreams of children,
        children for whom sex was still
                as genderless as the universe,
    the choppy bay waters, scaled and finned by light. Whatever
manner of creature she was those afternoons, it couldn't be human:
    Monster of the Bay, her puny limbs lengthening into tentacles.
    Secret
Demon of the Waters.
           Or God of the Dock, her body bared and
           pressed
to its warm damp planks, the dock
    creaking as it heaved beneath her, bleeding creosote — the heavy
    sexual reek
of creosote and bay and rot. Unforgettable. For every vice there are
    virtues. No? Here was a Vanity so thorough it excluded
        Impatience or Envy. Her brothers
           would share their catch
with her — sometimes fish,
        sometimes baskets of crabs, and then the small
        change
the man always gave for letting him do what he did on them, which hurt
    no more than the soft suck of tidal mud
hurt down there at low tide when they played being clams.

Percussion

For Jeff Barr

Or when birds fly smack into a window
by a feeder, mistaking the sky
it mirrors for actual sky.... That's what

it's like to mistake every polite
man for one's father. And the sound
their bodies make when they hit—

if one listens, really attends—not a thud,
not a thwack, but the percussion that follows
a blow to the belly, that ungh

when the wind gets knocked out
and the loud silence after.
Listen. Harder. Harder.

Coming Home from the Circus My Son Makes Me Promise Not to Say "Bear"

For Adam

Even if we say it under our breaths
    Or in our heads, they will hear us.
Called out of their privacy, believing
    We are their lost mothers
And only sons, they will find us.
    They will smell circus bear on our
Clothing. They will know
    Where we've been. Bear-mean,
They will carry us into the Pine
    Barrens. They will have us
Catch fish with our clumsy hands,
    Have us dance on all fours. Show us
Food, hide it, have us find it again
    By scent. They will unname us,
Cage us in unbearable freedoms.

Accidental Mercy

Ask her. Those days when she held her child-body like a burn
before the world's lips, who came?
—besides now and then a wind off the ocean, blowing, blowing,
in accidental mercy. Whose little brat was she
that her mouth should open

to these instruments, familiarly, as if they were her own
thumb? That her tongue requires no instruction? Ever.
Crazy old thing. Who brushed her hair?
Who soaped her body, releasing its tenderness
like a green scent? Whose hands, minty,

almost astringent, lathered the aches
that would become her breasts? Just whose little
friend was she, that she welcomes the needle? That prick
at her gum: a quick pleasure like salt-
grains in sea water piercing a skinned elbow long ago,

and then, the numbness: a thickness that hums
far under the drill? To welcome
the drill, and dentists, coming closer, no matter
her decay, and hygienists, likewise, with their trained
impersonality—like the ocean, like

wind, their arms brushing her breasts, their wrists
leaning in: skin to skin. Radical old woman.
Ask her why every indifferent touch is a stroke
she trusts, trusts and welcomes above passion.
Ask her again why she didn't want kids.

The Parents They Would Be

For M and M

old hippies
who could name us
the names of every apple
went into our sauces and butters and pies and cobblers and
    tarts and ciders
but don't

who pass slowly among
the fruits of our labor
as if there were all the time
and nothing better to do in this world than to praise
and to savor

Part Three

Half Note for Hayden

my friend John,
the peeping Tom,
would find us odd
and not a little,
for here I'll stand
and there you'll stand,
and there I'll stand
and here you'll stand,
a likely woman and
a likely man,
side by side
and all night long,
and not so much as cuddle,
but as two dark keys
that never touch
couple in a chord,
so we too struck
by God knows what,
Waller's boogies
or Morton's rolls,
Hot Lips' riffs
or Bessie's groans,
move in tune
and yet alone.

Poster Postnote: For Memoirs By Post-Plaster Caster, Post-Projective Verse, Post-Pop History Sisters

On one
tower of the World
Trade Center and then
the other. Or for hours
backstage at The Play-
house. In an abandoned
outhouse in Kansas; the
devil comes
from Kansas
and we did it
with the devil.
We did it once
in our father's
bed; twice
on the White
House lawn.
We did it at
a poetry fest;
it'd been done
before. On Wall
St., when it
was late and right;
on the outskirts
of Wall St., in
the middle of

                    rush hour, we
                  did it. In the cock-
                  pit of a Blackhawk,
                    on a mission
                   to Miami, we did it
                 in five   minutes,
                        flat.
     You got   the balls? Baby,
     we got   the gear —
     stopwatch,   scale and tape.
               Give it to us straight.

Why I'm Always Playing with My Hair, What This Has to Do with My Life

"My thumbs have always felt
ambivalent about my fingers.
I know this is hard to believe
but they're not really swingers,
they're monogamous right down
to their nails and can't understand
how the fingers handle so many affairs.
Sure they go to the fingers
when the fingers come to them
but the fingers never seem to need
the thumbs the way the thumbs
need the fingers. The thumbs
are certain the fingers are just
using them, and this hurts
but thumbs aren't the kind to complain.
Instead they grow a little neurotic,
have false pregnancies and often
fall cuticles over moons in love
with lean hungry index fingers.
I play with my hair, run thumb
and index, tip to tip, down the dark
strands, a shameless romantic.

I write to make my thumbs happy."

Of the Pleasures

The sag
of
this
and that
means less
for one
who's taken full
advantage
of the flesh
when it
was fresh.

Abishag: To the Tune of Fats Waller's "Rockin' Chair"

When, like a pair of kid gloves,
the mop handle fit Abishag's hands,
or like her last good man, perfectly,
and the hour, too, was perfect,
four or thereabouts in the AM,
the cabaret empty then, with everybody
headed for the after-hours tonks
except for her, the singing charwoman,
and for him, the stoned piano player,
taking her requests; when
her impossible fate would become
a lover whom she, most
unwillingly, forgave everything.

Muse Tune

Not during your meal,
or when your best old
friend scares you

by acting his age,
not while your spouse
is being beautiful

so that you're feeling humble
but later, while sipping
champagne and feeling it

like the first time
you snapped your fingers,
think of me then.

And toast the musicians.
I've slept with them too.
Their music will tell you

I am a mission, a phone booth,
other people's secrets
mature in my belly,

I am the daughters
you would like to know better,
nothing less than all

the lovers who have ever opened
under you; how left alone
I turn back into myself

and never hit bottom,
how like a good thing I am
always about to end.

February 14th, 1986

For RM

the snow last night
in flakes so fat and slow and grey
they could have been ashes
the world ending

in flames after all
while my young friend at the hospice
recited for me his final
pained couplet

where as innocently and prettily
as snow
in drifts sex proved
murderous

Intraterrestrials

The body alters more rapidly than a planet.
A hole in the lungs' upper atmosphere?
—no question of cause and effect. Here
a lover drowns in her own melt-off; here a brother
evaporates in the heat of his own atoms.
Everybody should almost die at least once
in a lifetime, my friend, the brain
tumor survivor, says. And it's true. In pain
the body is its own Mount Everest. Gobi of
the thorax, tropic of the abdomen, Antarctica
of the extremities. Yet there is no word
for *yes* among Pain's people. Even our dearest
bravest are involuntary explorers. Enough,
and the poles of the body reverse:
every wind blowing in the wrong
direction, the self can't find its feet. Thumb back
an eyelid, and the eye is all surface, its attention
concentrated on the depths. One thinks of the eyes
of fish. In there all fish are sharks. Off
with an arm, out with a belly. All flesh is meat
in the killer's ontology. Pain? Among sharks, only sharks
have feelings. It's on a distant planet
the ozone layer thins and thins.
Losing my hair was the most traumatic
experience of my life, complains a customer
in an ad for Rogaine. *Lucky him,*
whispers the man in bed B, between waves,
his body swelling wherever it doesn't shrink.
Odd what messages reach them.
There isn't another body in the world

that can feel my father's pain. Still as if our
feelings mattered, he strains to cover
his exposed testicles with his good hand.

Marilyn, Marilyn

Give me an old movie
where I'd know how to act,
where the end is the end
when it is the end, no searching
for just the right rope,
no special effects.
If there is a cliff
let me do it by cliff,
a river, if cold and swift,
let me take that.
If *I cannot live with him*
and cannot live without him, let that
be that. And give me mourners
who know how to act.
Have them throw black rice
at my casket and sing
the wedding songs backwards.
If my lover be known
let his presence go unnoticed,
let his shame be private
and blameless — no fools
mourning for what might have been,
but true mourners, respecters
of hard luck and facts.

Gall

To take me that way,
like gruel and straight
from the bowl;
to wipe your mouth
on the back of your hands,
to wipe your mouth
on your sleeves; to grunt
your grace, to burp
your thanksgiving, to sleep
in my arms as soundly
as a little pig—you, you
whom I loved for your soul.

Arrangements I

They would weave
    my hair   they would stew
        my marrow
bones   for soup   from my skull
          carve spoons
that would serve
        them for ages.

So when I'm finished
    I might
        be thoroughly used,

let the pebbles
        of my ankles
          and wrists
          rattle for infants like you
            for whom
for an instant   life will seem good

Abishag: Our Lady of Sorrows Rest Home, February 14, 1983

It's all one,
chocolate cherries
or sour gum,
one, then another,
then another one.
Christmas? Easter?
One, then another, then
another one,
a candied Christ
or a liquorish nun.
What's the difference?
It's all one,
Valentines and
what's become
of the appetites
I knew when young.
The seasons shift?
I shift.
From hip to hip
I crave nothing more
than bon-bons
and buttered rum, hot
buttered rum and
bon-bons, one,
then another,
then another one.

Part Four

The Princess and the Uzi

For Mary and Art

Forget Little Red Riding Hood, sweetie.
In Arizona the fifty or so
wolves and half-wolves my friend Mary rescued
sang hourly, from midnight to sunrise,
not steadily but regularly, moon or no
moon — their bays welling,
cresting, breaking over the high desert wastes
in exultant polyphonic waves, while she, she,
my dear friend, would merely stretch, roll over
and smile moronically in her sleep. Christ, what gives
with these women I love? Again, those nights
in Santa Cruz, as if the air itself
were wired for sound — the least tremor, the least
wind, amplified; my friend's own Hindu
cow bells, adding their coloratura
to the communal cacophony, or what struck me
as cacophony, as I'd reach for
the bedlamp, once more imagining an Uzi
— prepared to blast the next sonofabitching
chime that moved. Oh, when the big one hits
those bells will create such a heavenly din
the citizens of Santa Cruz won't notice
the difference between the music of this
sphere and the next. So, may they
rest in peace! Me, I prefer
the gossip of leaves; my wolves asleep, fast
asleep, conversing in the privacy
of touch, the way they do, crowded in a heap,

so the breath of one parts the fur
of another, while the breath of another
strokes its neighbor's ear. Nothing strange
these days, I suppose, that my friends
should sleep best with something warm
in the air, a body of noise to insulate the exposed
flesh of belly and neck, or that others of us
require dead silence, as if we need to hear
what's coming even in our sleep. Ah, those fairy tale
girls rescued by galants, only think
what they'd make of a woman who counts
wolves the way others count sheep! Myself
I love a man with dainty ears, an edgy insomniac,
my equal in nerve and fear, who defends
my sleep, tooth and claw, as I his
against the burglars of quiet, the hitmen of dreams.

Fort Western

In the fine cracks between flagstones that deck the court-
    yard of the Faculty Club at Stanford, clubfoot moss struggles
in miniature, squatting on residue water
     intended for pricey
                potted camelias and gardenias.

Once more the shabby old visiting poet kneels
    to greet the invader, as if
it were his nearest relation. At that institution of higher
    education, once more
                encroaching natives sneak to his rescue.

A Brood of Critics; A Mischief of Poets

For D.S.

How out-best faultless parents?—Your mother,
  The long-retired teacher who still took
Up every room she entered, standing by
  Our chairs even when she sat: the mistress

Of a grammar we never could master,
  Of classes we must pass and knew we would
Fail—our failures once more chalking our mouths
  Like ash through dinner, while her too bright, kindly

Voice of correction stung our faces with shame's
  Instant rash. Woe to you, my friend: No home
From school ever—and your Dad a preacher.
  The brood laments your genius for mischief?

—For you, it was write poems or crack safes!
  How blessed we felt by our parents' neglect.

Song for Adam

Trees, trees, my lovely boy,
By cut of leaf, by cast
Of bud and bloom and seed, by cut
Of leaf they speak their names,
Post-oak, Gingko, and Hickory,
Locusts, black and honey,
Chestnut and Cherry speak
Their names, and Maples,
Silver, Sugar, and Japanese,
And springlong and summerlong,
My lovely son, the trees
Which are not evergreens,
Elder and Elm, Aspen and Ash,
By cast of bud and bloom and seed,
By cut of leaf they speak
And the swish of wind on leaf is sweet,
Is lullaby and hymn, the swish of wind,
My lovely boy, on leaf
Of Butternut and Beech,
This leafsome, treeful litany
That speaks to us
Springlong and summerlong,
That cast of bud and bloom, and of thee,
My Adam, calling me outside
To see, to see.

Night Court at Solomon's

Say it's Mother
   Death
     who has him
      by the ankles
       and won't
        let go, while
         the Other
          who claims
           he's Hers,
            no question, pulls
             at his wrists.

              at his wrists.
            no question, pulls
           he's Hers
          who claims
         the Other
        let go, while
       and won't
      by the ankles
     who has him
   Death
Say it's Mother

Instead of You

Flaking paint
   and broken plaster; snow
 reaching
       for your throat, pocked

with ash, refuse, cancers, and nothing for it
   but another snort or toke....

More: more and more: always more,
   the gospel, according to Saint

Schwartz.

      Then bitter. Bitter
   by the library at Syracuse ("Fuck, pills,"
you said. "Next time
   I'm using a pistol.") — I thought

of Delmore Schwartz
   because I could not think of you.

Evening Star

Let his breath come
               hard
                    let his shoulders

kill him
    these late afternoons
        after his long illness

still he climbs
    the long hill out back
           through snow
              to his absent son's trailer

where he will sit for awhile
           with the old cat who gets
              lonely up there.

(What else?—with his son on the road
    week-in
        week-out.)

To change her water,
to clean her box
if needed, humbly, on all fours,
to feed her treats—in substance
no different from thousands
of manuscripts edited,
hundreds of blurbs written, letters
answered, hungers appeased....

He will remove his boots
                    just inside the door
                                taking care
as always
            not to make a mess
                                        then
        as always
                    steady his nerves
with a cigarette.

"Envy of the placid beasts
is a very widespread affliction
in this type of sadness,"
William James wrote in *The Varieties*
of Religious Experience.

                        Poetry? The old
cat's pleasure will warm him
                            halfway like heat
                                cast by an open
fireplace in a drafty hall
                    which falls
short
        which cannot quite
                            reach around
no matter how
        radiant—even at home
                in bed with his wife.

                                Snow
will have melted through
        his jeans to his calves. He will

remember then before
he leaves he must water his son's plants.

Or at the windbreak
halfway down
how he will count five
no six

male cardinals lighting
on a wild choke cherry
(getting it right   exactly)
this image he will carry

home for his wife
who will be watching
for him down there

in the little red house
with its huge bird feeder
and neatly

stacked half-cord
at which he will be stopping first
to gather more wood
while there's still light.

Night Gardening

in that patch of low woods
   where the great white and snow
trilliums bloom I prepared

   this bed with a runcible spoon—
dreams
   just roomy enough

for an interim grave sanctuary or vacation
   spot among the threading roots
of red maple and fire cherry

   In place of you   a stick
fallen from our injured sycamore
   I sleeved in a strip of your once

favorite once green workshirt
   For me   a twig of witch hazel
spooled in a rag of still blue silk—

   I wanted a dream
location where we could retreat
   like bulbs overwintering

tubers or rhizomes freed of sun
   Oh not long   just time   enough
to let life die back a little

Don't Explain

You see
    Me married to a man much
Older than I am, and you wonder, you cannot
    Help yourself, you're human, you
Wonder: maybe this, maybe that, something
    Wrong here — and, my friends
I do not blame you, but sadly our story
    Is as pedestrian and
As grievous as most couples'
    Who've joined together in sickness
And in love to fight
    The good fight against history
And its awful successes
    For which
Age is the least difference we have
    To overcome.

Aubade

Under a broad red wing of maple
a broad-assed, fine-feathered Bacchus
dreaming it off or perhaps dreamless —
his figure, through the rain,
swimming free of family and genus, becoming
for a moment magnificent:
a great West Indian Nightwing,
twenty shades of black lightning in his tail.

In a lot behind Tut Jackson's High Hat Lounge,
about five maybe six this morning,
rocked to my knees, rocked into song
by this bloated old wreck of a boozer.

Ah, my love! My people, still? And after all and after all,
this desire to redeem you and to idolize you?

Acknowledgments

Grateful acknowledgment is made to the editors of the following publications in which these works, or earlier versions of them, previously appeared:

American Letters & Commentary: "The Princess and the Uzi."

Calapooya Collage: "Abishag: Our Lady of Sorrows Rest Home, February 14th, 1983," "Existentially Speaking."

Crazy Horse: "Across the Green," "Loose Children."

Exile: "Complicated," "Introit.," "Nearly,"

The Exquisite Corpse: "Black Irish Blues" as "Ms. Murphy, To You," "Prison."

Faultline: "On Instinct," "Psalm of Romona," "Why I'm Always Playing with My Hair, What This Has to Do with My Life."

The Georgia Review: "Black Irish Blues" as "Companion Pieces, I & II."

Graham House Review: "Percussion."

Harvard Magazine: "Hush."

Many Mountains Moving: "Aubade," "Don't Explain."

The New Review: "February 14th, 1986."

Ploughshares: "Ancient Francesca."

Poetry: "A Brood of Critics; A Mischief of Poets," "Coming Home From the Circus My Son Makes Me Promise Not to Say 'Bear,'" "Evening Star," "Fort Western," "Half Note for Hayden," "Muse Tune," "Night Court at Solomon's," "The Parents They Would Be," "Practice," "Abishag: To the Tune of Fats Waller's 'Rockin Chair."

Poetry East: "Gall."

Shenandoah: "Home Sickness."

Southern Poetry Review: "Marilyn, Marilyn" as "The End."

The following poems were previously published under the title, *Banshee Diaries*, Exile Editions, Toronto, Canada: "Introit," "Home Sickness," "Black Irish Blues," "Nearly," "Abishag's Brag," "Ms. Murphy, To You," "Existentially Speaking," "Ancient Francesca," "Prison," "Abishag Enjoins Her Cats to Eat," "Hush," "Complicated," "Abishag Confronts Her Mirror After a Stroll," "On Instinct," "Bad Medicine," "Across the Green," "Psalm of Ramona," "Emergency Measures," "Loose Children," "Percussion," "Coming Home From the Circus, My Son Makes Me Promise Not to Say 'Bear'," "Accidental

Mercy," "The Parents They Would Be," "Half Note for Hayden," "Poster Postnote : For Memoirs by Post-Plaster Caster, Post-Projective Verse, Post-Pop History Sisters," "Why I'm Always Playing with My Hair, What This Has to Do with My Life," "Of the Pleasures," "Abishag: To the Tune of Fats Waller's 'Rockin Chair'," "Muse Tune," "February 14th, 1986," "Marilyn, Marilyn," "Gall," "Abishag: Our Lady of Sorrows Rest Home, February 14th, 1983," "The Princess and the Uzi," "Fort Western," "Night Court at Solomon's," "Instead of You," "Evening Star," "Don't Explain," "Aubade."

Thanks to all my teachers and other beloveds. They know who they are and they know my gratitude. Still, I will name a few: Isabel Bizé, Philip Booth, Mary Bellis, Hayden Carruth, Claire and Barry Calaghan, Dr. Robert Daly, Stephen Dobyns, Stephen Dunn, Sam and Sally Green, Brooks Haxton, Jo Anne Pagono, Adrienne Rich, Jean Valentine, and Janet and Baron Wormser. No end.

"Ancient Francesca," as "Great Aunt Francesca," also appeared in the *Push-cart Prize Anthology, VIII,* and in the *Ploughshares Poetry Reader,* 1986. "Black Irish Blues" appeared in the anthology *Outsiders: Poems about Rebels, Exiles, and Renegades* (Milkweed Editions). I give thanks for fellowships from the New Jersey State Council on the Arts and for the Tietjens Memorial Prize from the Modern Poetry Assoiciation. I also want to thank Barry Calaghan, publisher of Exile Editions, Toronto, Ontario, for reprint rights to *The Banshee Diaries,* 1998. And for the republication of poems from *Black Irish Blues,* I warmly thank Sally and Sam Green of Brooding Heron Press, Waldron Island, WA.

About the Author

Joe-Anne McLaughlin was educated at Stockton State College and Syracuse University. Her honors include an Academy of American Poets Award, a Pushcart Prize, two fellowships from the New Jersey State Council on the Arts, and the 1993 Tietjens Memorial Prize awarded by *Poetry* magazine.

A college writing instructor for many years, she has also worked widely in community arts education, most recently conducting poetry writing workshops at the Rome Art and Community Center in Rome, New York, and at The Frost Place in Franconia, New Hampshire. She was a resident writer at The Poets' House in Clonbarra, Ireland, during the summer of 1998. In addition, she serves as a Communitiy Support Specialist for the disabled with Alternative Vocational Services, a non-profit agency in upstate New York.

BOA Editions, LTD.:
American Poets Continuum Series

Colophon

The publication of this book was made
possible, in part, by the special support of the
following individuals:

Nancy & Alan Cameros
Dr. William & Shirley Ann Crosby
Dane & Judy Gordon
Richard Garth & Mimi Hwang
Susan DeWitt Davie, Deb & Kip Hale
William Hauser, Peter & Robin Hursh,
Robert & Willy Hursh
Fred & Rose-Marie Klipstein
Archie & Pat Kutz, Gert Niers
Boo Poulin, Deborah Ronnen
Peggy Savlov, Pat & Michael Wilder
Helen & Glenn Williams
Milton Wood

This book was set in New Caledonia designed
by W.A. Dwiggins, with titles in Nofret
designed by Gudrun Zapf-Von Hesse.

The interior was designed by
Valerie Brewster, Scribe Typography.

The cover was designed by Geri McCormick.
Cover art: *Phoenix,* by Martha Ward,
courtesy of Constance Ashton Myers.

Manufacturing was by McNaughton & Gunn,
Saline, Michigan.